Christmas Plays for Children:

4 Biblical Plays to Celebrate the Christmas Season

Dawyn Sawyer

TRILOGY

Trilogy Christian Publishers

A Wholly Owned Subsidiary of Trinity Broadcasting Network

2442 Michelle Drive

Tustin, CA 92780

For information, address Trilogy Christian Publishing

Rights Department, 2442 Michelle Drive, Tustin, Ca 92780.

Trilogy Christian Publishing/ TBN and colophon are trademarks of Trinity Broadcasting Network.

For information about special discounts for bulk purchases, please contact Trilogy Christian Publishing.

Manufactured in the United States of America

10 9 8 7 6 5 4 3 2 1

Library of Congress Cataloging-in-Publication Data is available.

ISBN 979-8-88738-703-1

ISBN 979-8-88738-704-8 (ebook)

Table of Contents

Introduction

One of my favorite Christmas activities is helping with the children's Christmas play each year at church. I enjoy watching the children dress up in silly costumes and sing Christmas songs with much gusto as the parents watch their children with such pride on the stage. The practices are usually terrible, with many mistakes, but the enthusiasm of the children is always infectious. When it comes to the final performance, my view is that the more mistakes they make, the better I like it! This is not a Broadway production; it is a profound truth told by children through storytelling.

I have taught Sunday school for many years, and it always seems to be a chore to come up with something new and exciting for a Christmas program every year. I feel blessed to have created these Christmas plays, with the Lord's help, that try to tell the story from different perspectives of the story's characters while keeping true to the central theme. Writing gives me an opportunity to reflect on the simple yet profound truths of the Christmas story; God became man, born as an infant. He was born not in the comforts of the local hospital but rather, in a barn, with angelic beings heralding his entry. The angels declared the birth to the shepherds, the rejected class of men, who believed the message and told others about this unusual birth. Seekers, the Magi, came to worship the child while Herod tried to destroy him. The story never gets old!

It is my hope and prayer that you will use these Christmas plays as an opportunity to share the Christmas story in a fun way with your church and community.

Enjoy! 2 John 2

Dawyn Sawyer

General Notes

When to Start Practicing

If possible, I recommend starting to plan for your Christmas program in August, when you start your fall Sunday school schedule. If the Christmas program is built into your schedule, you are more likely to have the support of the other Sunday school teachers and be able to plan for the practices needed during the Sunday school hour as you get closer to Christmas. I recommend setting aside some time each week to learn the songs in November and then adding additional time for the play script practice during the month of December, depending on when you plan to have the production. You can consider a few Saturday morning dress rehearsals the day before your final performance. Be sure to have some Christmas snacks to thank them for all their hard work! Many churches hold the children's Christmas play the Sunday before Christmas. It really doesn't matter; what matters is that the children (and adult family members) are given the opportunity to be involved in this church tradition and to be reminded of the real reason that we celebrate Christmas: the birth of Jesus.

If time is short, these plays can be performed with only a few practices or without any practices at all. Just hand out the scripts to whoever shows up, assign the parts, and let it fly. It's all good.

How to Divide up the Parts

As with any play, you must consider the number and ages of the children in your program so that each one of them can have at least one speaking part if they are able to read and wish to contribute. Considering this, the major roles can be divided among two or even three persons to share parts. Lesser roles can also be split between two children. Even if a child is shy and does not want to speak, encourage them to be up on the stage, participating at their level of comfort. If you have a shortage of children, I recommend that you encourage the teens and parents in your church to work alongside the younger children to put on the play. This does raise the standard of performance but can still provide an opportunity for the younger children to dress up and role-play, which is what they want. Just make it fun!

The Scripts

It is entirely optional to have the children memorize the scripts. There is usually limited time to prepare and practice for the performance, so having the sheets with large print (16 to 20 font) helps everyone to read their part more easily. Plan to have a script printed off for each child to hold. Clearly mark out each part by highlighting each part and writing the name of the part and student on the top of the first page. In each script, italicized words are used to give direction to the reader to emphasize that word or phrase. At other times, stage directions are given in parentheses to guide readers on how to speak the words that follow or to give specific directions. Even if a child may not be able to be there for the final performance, please let all children participate in any practices you have. It is important that each child who attends your Sunday school program feels loved and a part of the program, no matter what their life circumstances. Those that may not be able to come to the final performance are often those who need the love of Jesus the most! Be sure to gather all paper copies up at the end of each practice to avoid losing them for future practice sessions. Feel free to mark them up with hints and help for each child.

The Stage Setting

It is not essential to have a special stage setting for any of these plays. If you can put up a painted sheet with a simple sky design on the wall behind the stage area, that is sufficient. If not, just use the wall that you have; everyone will be looking at the children anyway. To help with floor staging, put some pieces of tape on the floor to mark out where you want the children to stand. If you can set up one or two spotlights, it may help to add a dramatic touch, but it is not necessary for the performance. Microphones and other sound equipment technology *are* essential for the performance, as the acoustics in many church buildings are inadequate for the soft voices of children who are shy on stage.

Costumes

Costumes for a Christmas play do not have to be extravagant or expensive. Old draperies, sheets and towels, and bathrobes have been used to make floor-length clothes that were common in Jesus' day. Rope belts can be used to tie up waists and headpieces. Tea towels and hand towels make great headpieces for shepherds and Joseph. A long thin sheer curtain can be used for Mary's headpiece. Crowns can be made for the Magi by covering cardboard with aluminum foil and gluing on simple beads or play jewels. If you do not have special costumes, do not worry, the audience will be listening to the parts.

Having the preschool class dress up as angels, shepherds, or animals is usually a fun way for them to be a part of your program if you have sufficient numbers. They are always the best part of the play, and the parents love it!

Songs and Music

Songs are not required but are certainly enjoyed by children and adults. I have provided suggestions for the songs we used when performing, but feel free to change the songs to suit your circumstances. One of the plays was written during the covid pandemic, and singing was not allowed in the UK, where I was living, so no songs were part of the original performance. If you have only a few children in your congregation, let them sing the first verse of your chosen songs, then have the congregation join in for the remaining verses. Adults love to participate, also! You can ask the children to memorize the songs if they have enough time, or you can use a music sheet with each of the songs printed out for children who read to use. Please see those provided in the appendix for my suggested songs. Print off plenty of these sheets to use during practice times and send them home so parents can help the kids learn the words. Be sure to save enough for the performance. It does not matter if you use live music or pre-recorded background music. Either will work, depending on your circumstances and available resources.

Remember, there is no right or wrong way to do the play. Just have fun and let the story be told by the children of your local church!

Role/student: ____________________________

Play One: From the Hillside

Scene One	Scene Two	Scene Three
Oldest Shepherd	Youngest shepherd	Oldest Shepherd
Youngest Shepherd	Old shepherd 2	Youngest shepherd
Old shepherd 2	Oldest Shepherd	Old shepherd 2
Old shepherd 3	Angel	Old shepherd 3
Angel	Mary & Joseph	Wise men
	Host of Angels	

Scene One: *A number of shepherds are out in the fields around Bethlehem one summer morning. The oldest shepherd is very old and is teaching the younger ones how to do their jobs.*

Stage directions: *The lights from the city of Bethlehem are seen off in the distance. Shepherds spend most of their time on the right side of the stage. Other characters come in and out of the left side of the stage as events are re-enacted in the play.*

Oldest Shepherd: Remember, when you go to find a lamb, be very careful to let the mother sheep know that this is their lamb, or they will not continue to take care of it.

Youngest shepherd: You sure know a lot about how to raise sheep, Uncle. Have you been a shepherd for a very long time?

Oldest Shepherd: Yes, it has been a very long time. I have seen a lot of things in my lifetime.

Old shepherd 2: It's certainly going to be a long night, brother. Tell us a story. Do you remember *that night*? Tell us again about what happened that night so long ago.

Oldest Shepherd: Yes, that night was so different from any other night that I remember. How could anyone forget? I was about as old as you are, my nephew. I was so excited to finally be old enough to stay out with the sheep at night. We were out in the fields, a night like tonight. We had just rounded up all the sheep and put them in the pen for the night. It was a clear dark night. *(With emphasis)* When suddenly, the angel of the Lord appeared. He was bright white and lit up the sky.

(First angel comes to the right side of the stage)

Old shepherd 3: We didn't know what to think. Remember, some of the shepherds started to run away. They were so frightened.

Old shepherd 2: I also remember that something stopped us dead in our tracks. Do you remember what it was?

Oldest Shepherd: Yes, the angel spoke to us.

Youngest shepherd: What did he say?

(Angel steps up to the front of the stage)

Angel: Do not be afraid. I bring you good news of great joy that will be for all the people.

Oldest Shepherd: *(quietly, to himself)* Good news, the gospel, the gospel.

Youngest shepherd: *(looking at the oldest shepherd)* What did he mean, Uncle?

Oldest Shepherd: Well, at that time, we were not sure. The word gospel means good news. But the angel continued:

Angel: Today, in the town of David, a Savior has been born to you. He is Christ the Lord.

Song suggestion: Hark the Herald Angels Sing

Scene Two:

Youngest shepherd: What did he mean when he said, "the town of David?"

Old shepherd 2: That means Bethlehem. That is the town where King David was born, and it is often referred to as the city of David.

Youngest shepherd: What did he mean, a Savior?

Old shepherd 2: Well, we have always known that we need someone to save us. David wrote a song, "God is my rock, my shield, my refuge and my Savior," when God continually saved him while King Saul kept trying to kill him all those years he was king *(2 Samuel 22:3)*.

Youngest shepherd: What else did the angel say?

Oldest Shepherd: He said there would be a sign.

Angel: You will find a baby wrapped in rags and lying in a manger.

(Angel departs quietly stage left)

Youngest shepherd: In a manger? That's not where babies should be born.

Old shepherd 2: As I remember, there was something special about that year. Do you remember? Which year was it?

Oldest Shepherd: Yes, that was the year that Caesar Augustus issued some kind of decree to tax the people. He wanted everyone to return to the home of their ancestors so he could tax the cities and towns. There was a young couple named Mary and Joseph who were both from the lineage of David and had to travel all the way from Nazareth down to Bethlehem. They had to travel slowly because Mary was pregnant with her first child. By the time they got to Bethlehem, the town was filled with all kinds of hustle and bustle from so many people. The town seemed to be bursting at the seams. Every inn was filled up; every home had relatives who were staying with them because of the census.

Youngest shepherd: So where did Mary and Joseph stay? Did they have relatives in town?

Stage direction: *Mary and Joseph knock on a door as in a mime. The innkeeper says nothing; he points to the stables and shakes his head yes. He then closes the door. Mary and Joseph go and sit down at the stables.*

Oldest Shepherd: That was a problem, as I remember. All the inns were full. Finally, someone said that they could sleep out with the animals at the stable if they wanted to. That night Mary had her baby right there *(pause for 2–3 seconds and speak slowly)* in—the—stable.

Song suggestion: Away in A Manger

Youngest shepherd: What happened next, Uncle?

Oldest Shepherd: Well, of course, we did not understand everything that happened. *(Pause, as if remembering)* Then suddenly, up in the sky, a whole host of angels appeared, praising God.

(Angels walk in, to side of the stage. Stand ready to speak)

Youngest shepherd: *(With great excitement, looking at the angels)* What did they say?

Host of Angels *(all together in unison)* Glory to God in the Highest, and on earth, peace, goodwill to men!

Song suggestion: Angels we have heard on High

(Angels leave the stage quietly as they came in)

Scene Three:

Old shepherd 2: They left as suddenly as they came and went back up into heaven.

Youngest shepherd: That must have been really exciting to see.

Oldest Shepherd: Yes, it was, but it was also frightening too. We all sat around the fire, afraid to speak. We were all thinking to ourselves, "Did I really see that? What just happened?" "What does it mean?"

Oldest Shepherd: Finally, my brother, your Uncle Ben said, "Let's go to Bethlehem and see if this really happened. You know, what the Lord just told us about." So, we hurried off to town and searched for the baby. We weren't sure which stable to look in, but finally, we found Mary, Joseph, and the new baby lying in a manger, just like the angel said.

Old shepherd 2: It was so exciting to see the Christ child! Mary asked how we knew they were there, and my brother told them about the angels.

You could see Mary was treasuring all these things in her heart and pondering it all.

Old Shepherd 3: We were so excited that we did not go straight back to the fields. As the morning sun was coming up, we told everyone in town what we saw. We spread the news to everyone!

Song suggestion: Go Tell it on the Mountain

Old shepherd 2: The people were very amazed at what we told them.

Oldest Shepherd: Early in the morning, we returned to the fields; we were praising God and giving Him lots of glory for all the things we had seen and heard. It was awesome. Everything the angels said had come true.

Youngest shepherd: That must have been really exciting to be the first ones to see this baby! Did anyone ever see this baby again?

(Wise men dressed up come to a house and give gifts to Mary and Joseph. They bow down in worship)

Oldest Shepherd: Yes, some Magi from the East came to Jerusalem and spoke with King Herod because they saw the star in the sky that told of the promise. They were asking everyone where the king of the Jews was because they saw the star in the sky. They came a long way to worship him. They remembered that in the Scripture, the Christ child would come out of Bethlehem.

Wise Men *(in unison)*: But you, Bethlehem, in the land of Judah, are by no means least among the rulers of Judah; for out of you will come a ruler who will be the shepherd of my people Israel *(Micah 5:2)*.

Song suggestion: O Little Town of Bethlehem

Old shepherd 2: I think I heard that Herod asked them to come back and tell them if they found the child. Later, we heard that Herod was furious, stating that the Magi had tricked him. They did not go back and speak with Herod. The story goes that they gave the child gifts of gold, frankincense, and myrrh. Then an angel warned them not to go back to Herod, so they went home another route. It was shortly after that when

Herod put out the decree to kill all the baby boys under two years of age, at the time the star appeared in the sky. We always wondered if the family was able to escape harm.

Youngest shepherd: Christmas is certainly a time of great celebration. We remind ourselves every year that the little baby Jesus was born in a manger.

Oldest Shepherd: Yes, Christmas is a time for joy. We celebrate each year the joy of God sending His Son to save all mankind. It certainly is something to celebrate. Join us all in singing: Joy to the World.

Song suggestion: Joy to the World.

Stage direction: *All take a bow!*

Needs for the Play

Title: **From the Hillside**

[ ] Date of performance: ______________________

[ ] Dates for Practice: ____

Major Roles	**Student**	**Alternate**	**Comments**
Oldest shepherd			
Old shepherd 2			
Old shepherd 3			
Youngest shepherd			
Young shepherd 2			
Young shepherd 3			
Minor roles			
Angel			
Mary			
Joseph			
Wise men			

[ ] Scripts printed off for children and adult leaders. The number needed: ______________

Additional needs for performance:

Stage/Lightening/sound:

[ ] costumes

[ ] microphones/ lighting, etc.

[ ] stage props, etc.

Songs/ Music:

[ ] Songs chosen

[ ] Music given to person organizing

[ ] one-page sheet written up for students

Who needs to know:

[ ] Confirm date with church calendar

[ ] Notice to parents

[ ] Advertisement to church and community

Role/student: ______________________

Play Two: One Starry Night

Scene One	Scene Two	Scene Three
Old Star	3 young stars	Old Star
3 young stars	Old Star	Angel of the Lord
Angel Gabriel	Angel Gabriel	Host of Angels
Old Angel	Mary	Simeon
Zechariah	Angel of the Lord	Wise men
		Chief Priest
		Young star

***Scene**: The stage is set with a night sky and a Jewish village seen off in the distance. One bright star is shining above the city of Bethlehem.*

***Stage direction:** The Old stars enter the stage, with young stars sitting down and looking up at the old stars. Choir comes forth to sing the first song, then recedes into the background before the characters of scene one start their lines.*

***Song suggestion**: It Came Upon a Midnight Clear*

Scene One:

Old Star: *(looking at the young stars seated on the floor)* As stars, we shine in the sky every night. Even if it rains, we stars are there to guide people home. Our constellations are known all over the world.

Yes—until electricity was invented, people used to be guided by us for all kinds of travel. It could be very dark on earth if the moon were not up in the sky.

Stars have always guided people in their travels. Do you remember that year long ago when the special star, *the star of Bethlehem,* guided the special group of men to the baby, Jesus?

Of course, at that time, they did not fully understand the significance of that star. In fact, most people did not even notice it. But *some* knew something special was foretold, so they decided to follow the star, those wise men from the East, the Magi.

Young Star 1: Tell us more, Uncle.

Young star 2: Yes, Uncle. What happened so long ago?

Old star: Well, it was a night like tonight. As the sun was just setting over the earth, one of our special stars began to shine over the small town of Bethlehem in the land of a country called Israel. We had not seen this star before, so we were all trying to figure out what it meant. As we were pondering, the angel Gabriel appeared.

(Angel Gabriel and Zachariah enter the stage)

Old Star: What have you been up to?

Angel Gabriel: I have been visiting the earth. God gave me some special messages to deliver. I think something very special is going to happen very soon.

Young star 1: What do you mean? Something special?

Angel Gabriel: Well, God had me appear to a High Priest named Zechariah when he was burning incense in the temple. I certainly scared him! I told him he would have a son, even though he and his wife were very old. He was skeptical and did not believe me, so God made him speechless until the baby was born. He had lots of time to think about his disbelief. By the time his baby was born, he really understood what was happening. He knew his son would be a prophet for God. But even more importantly, he understood that God was sending another special person, the redeemer, the Messiah.

Old Angel: After the birth of his son, Zechariah said—

Zechariah: Praise be to the Lord, the God of Israel because He has come and has redeemed his people! He has raised up a horn of salvation for us in the house of his servant David *(Luke 1:68)*.

Scene Two

3 Young stars: *(each star asks a question rapidly without waiting for the answer)* What is a redeemer? What is a horn of salvation? What does Messiah mean?

Old Star: Slow down; not so many questions?

A *redeemer* is a kinsman who buys back the land, such as in the story of Ruth.

The *horn of salvation* is someone who will rescue the people. Like Moses rescued the Israelites from Egypt.

Messiah is a Jewish word that means the *Anointed One*, someone set apart for God's special purposes.

Angel Gabriel: Not long after that first visit to Zechariah, God sent me to a Jewish girl by the name of Mary.

(Mary enters on the other side of the stage and looks at the Angel Gabriel)

Angel Gabriel: Greetings, you who are highly favored! The Lord is with you. *(Now speaking to the audience)* You could see Mary was really troubled by my words and was trying to figure out what it all meant. So, I continued. *(turn back and speak to Mary)*

Angel Gabriel: Do not be afraid, Mary. You have found favor with God. You will be with child and give birth to a son, and you are to give him the name Jesus. He will be great and will be called the Son of the Most High. The Lord God will give him the throne of his father David, and he will reign over the house of Jacob forever; his kingdom will never end.

Mary: *(Looking very confused)* How will this be, since I am a virgin?

Angel Gabriel: The Holy Spirit will come upon you, and the power of the Most High will overshadow you. So, the holy one to be born will be called the Son of God.

Angel Gabriel *(continuing)***:** Even Elizabeth, your relative, is going to have a child in her old age, and she, who was said to be barren, is in her sixth month. *(pause for emphasis)* For *nothing is impossible* with God.

Old Star: Mary's response was very different from Zechariah's. She said:

Mary: I am the Lord's servant. May it be to me as you have said.

(Mary leaves the stage. After she leaves, the Star turns to the audience and continues)

Old Star: Mary went to visit her relative, Elizabeth. When she returned home, you could tell she was pregnant. Joseph found out and was very confused. He could not believe that Mary could do something so shameful. So, he decided that he would quietly divorce her to avoid public disgrace, but then, the Angel of the Lord appeared to him in a dream and told him:

Angel of the Lord: Joseph, son of David, do not be afraid to take Mary home as your wife because what is conceived in her is from the Holy Spirit. She will give birth to a son, and you are to give him the name Jesus because he will save his people from their sins.

Old Star: When Joseph woke up, he believed the Angel and took Mary as his wife.

Young star: What does the name Jesus mean?

Old Star: Jesus is the Greek form of the name Joshua, which means the Lord saves. *(Turn now and speak to the audience)*

Old Star: The same year before Jesus was born, Caesar Augustus issued a decree that a census should be taken of the entire Roman World. Everyone had to go to his own town to register. So, Joseph also went up from the town of Nazareth in Galilee to Judea, to Bethlehem, the town of David, because he belonged to the house and line of David.

Old Star: He went there to register with Mary, who was pledged to be married to him and was expecting a child.

While they were there in Bethlehem, the time came for the baby to be born, and she gave birth to her firstborn, a son. She wrapped him in cloths and placed him in a manger because there was no room for them in the inn.

Song Suggestion: Away in a Manger

Scene Three

Old star: The night the baby Jesus was born, the angel of the Lord appeared to shepherds out in the fields around Bethlehem. Of course, they were terrified and confused: What could it all mean?

But the angel answered them—

Angel of the Lord: Do not be afraid. I bring you good news of great joy that will be for all the people. Today in the town of David, a Savior has been born to you; he is Christ the Lord.

This will be a sign to you: You will find a baby wrapped in cloths and lying in a manager.

Old Star: Suddenly, a great company of the heavenly host appeared with the Angel of the Lord, praising God and saying—

Host of angels: *(all together in unison)* Glory to God in the highest, and on earth, peace to men on whom his favor rests.

Old Angel: After we went back up into heaven, the shepherds went into town and found the baby Jesus, just like we said; they told everyone about the night and praised and worshiped God.

Old Angel: After the baby was born, they took him to Jerusalem to perform the purification rites according to the Law of Moses. When they were there, they saw a man called Simeon. He was an old man who was righteous and devout. The Holy Spirit had told him that he would not die before he saw the Lord's Christ.

When he saw the baby Jesus, he knew that He was the promised child.

(Simeon comes onto the stage and speaks to the audience.)

Simeon: *(speaking to the audience)* Sovereign Lord, as you have promised, you now dismiss your servant in peace. For my eyes have seen your salvation, which you have prepared in the sight of all people, a light for revelation to the Gentiles and for glory to your people Israel. *(Exit stage)*

Old Star: From what we understand, Mary and Joseph stayed in Bethlehem for several years after his birth. About two years later, a group of wise men from the East, called the Magi, came to Jerusalem and asked:

(Wise men, Herod, and Chief Priest enter)

Wise men: *(in unison)* Where is the one who has been born king of the Jews? We saw his star in the east and have come to worship him.

Old Star: Well, King Herod heard about their inquiry and was very disturbed. He summoned the chief priests and teachers of the Law and asked, "Where will Christ be born?"

Chief Priest: But you, Bethlehem, in the land of Judah, are by no means least among the rulers of Judah; for out of you will come a ruler who will be the shepherd of my people Israel.

Old Star: Herod secretly called the Magi and found the exact time the star had appeared. He told the Magi to go and search for the child and come report back to him.

The Magi followed the star, and it stopped over the house where the family lived. They bowed down and worshiped Jesus. They opened their treasures and presented him with gifts of gold, incense, and myrrh.

They were warned in a dream not to go back to Herod, so they returned to their county by another route.

(Exit Wise men, Herod and Chief Priest)

Old Star continues: When they had gone, an angel of the Lord appeared to Joseph in a dream and told him: Get up and take the child and his mother and escape to Egypt. Stay there until I tell you, for Herod is going to search for the child to kill him.

Young star: What is so special about this baby Jesus who was born in a manger?

Old Star: That question is still being asked today.

For those who know Him, He is the Promised One of God and the Savior of the world.

For those who do not know Him, He is just a story.

It is my hope that you will see this Jesus as God who became a man so that we could come back to God. As our sinful nature separates us from God, it is *His great love* for us that He chose to provide the solution for our sins. We can do nothing. He does it all. All we have to do is believe in what God has already done! But that, my little star, is another story!

Needs for the Play

Title: **One Starry Night**

[ ] Date of performance: ______________________

[ ] Date of practices: ____

Role	Student	Alternate	comments
Old star			
Young star			
Another star			
Angel Gabriel			
Zechariah			
3 young stars			
Mary			
Angel of the Lord			
Host of Angels			
Simeon			
Wise men			
Chief Priest			

[ ] Scripts printed off for children and adult leaders. The number needed: ______________

Additional needs for performance:

Stage/Lightening/sound:

[ ] costumes

[ ] microphones/ lighting, etc.

[ ] stage props, etc.

Songs/ Music:

[ ] Songs chosen

[ ] Music given to person organizing

[ ] one-page sheet written up for students

Who needs to know:

[ ] Confirm date with church calendar

[ ] Notice to parents

[ ] Advertisement to church and community

Role/student: ______________________

Play Three: God Keeps His Promise

Scene One	Scene Two	Scene Three
Child 1/2/3	Child 1/2	
Narrator 1	Narrator 1/3	Narrator 1/3
Narrator 2	Narrator 2/4	Narrator 2/4
God	Isaiah	Micah
Abraham	Angel Gabriel	Baalam
	Mary	Nathan

Scene One: *Children on stage looking at a Nativity in the corner of the stage.*

***Stage direction**: Have all ages of the children up on stage to sing the first song; then have the pre-school children go to their seats with their parents after the first song.*

Song suggestion: Away in A Manger

Child 1: Why do people put up a Nativity when we celebrate Christmas?

Child 2: Who was the baby Jesus? He was born so long ago.

Child 3: Why is he important in the Christmas celebration today?

Narrator 1: *(Speaking to the children)* Those are great questions! Everyone should ask themselves why they should celebrate Christmas. They need to understand that the Nativity, the birthplace of Jesus, is the central theme of Christmas, although many times, it seems to be forgotten. No matter how we celebrate Christmas, in God's mind, the birth of Jesus is the fulfillment of a promise that He made long ago. And in His perfect time, He kept that promise!

Narrator 1: *(Now turning to the audience)* Jesus fulfills so many of the prophecies regarding the promised Messiah to the Jewish nation. There are just too many circumstances in his birth, in his ministry, and in his death that were prophesied regarding the Messiah. This was more than a mere coincidence. God planned this all along!

Child 2: But what do you mean?

Child 3: Why do we need a promise? Why do we need a Messiah?

Narrator 2: Well, From the very beginning, God made man in His image. When Adam and Eve ate the forbidden fruit and sinned, He had to remove them from the Garden of Eden. But, even then, God already had a plan to bring mankind back to Himself. He gave curses to each one; the curse to the serpent tells us much about what God thinks of sin:

God: I will put enmity between you and the woman and between your offspring and hers; he will crush your head, and you will strike his heel. *(Genesis 3:15)*

Narrator 1: Because man's hearts are evil, they do not really want God's best for their lives. Throughout history, men have always tried to do things their own way. But God's way is very different from ours. So, He decided to work a plan through Abram. God promised Abram that he would have a son, but it was twenty-five years before this came true. And just before his son was born, God changed his name to Abraham, which means father of many *(Genesis 17:5)*.

One day, when this special son was older, God told Abraham:

God: Take your son, your only son, Isaac, whom you love, and go to the region of Moriah. Sacrifice him there as a burnt offering on one of the mountains I will tell you about *(Genesis 22:2)*.

Narrator 2: So, Abraham did as God told him, and as he placed his son Isaac on the altar, Isaac asked where the lamb was for the sacrifice. Abraham's response showed great faith as he said:

Abraham: *(speaking to audience)* God himself will provide the lamb for the burnt offering, my son.

Narrator 2: And, indeed, He did. A ram was caught by the horns in a thicket, and he became the burnt offering instead of Isaac. Because of Abraham's obedience, even though it seemed like an impossible act to expect Abraham to kill his own son, he figured that God would have to raise him from the dead *(Hebrews 11:19)* because he believed the promises that God told him regarding his descendants, who were not yet born. Because of his belief, God promised that He would bless him and make his descendants as numerous as stars in the sky. And that, through his offspring, all nations on earth would be blessed because of his obedience *(Genesis 22:18)*.

So, you see, God keeps His promises. He has always had Christmas on His mind.

Song suggestion: O Come, all ye Faithful

Scene Two

Child 1: I still don't understand. How is the Nativity part of God's plan?

Narrator 1/3: Well, you see, in the Bible, there are lists of descendants of Abraham, and Jesus is listed in them. Both Matthew and Luke, books in the New Testament, show that Jesus is a descendant of Abraham. And so, the birth of Jesus is the fulfillment of this Promise.

Narrator 2/4: (*Turn and speak to the Audience*) Today, let's just look at the birth of Jesus and see how God arranged this to fulfill this promise.

In the Old Testament, the prophet Isaiah declared that God will do something for the people of Israel because of their lack of faith:

Isaiah: The Lord himself will give you a sign: A virgin will be with child and will give birth to a son and will call him Immanuel *(Isaiah 7:14)*.

Narrator 2/4: Later, he says this of this same special child:

Isaiah: For to us a child is born, to us, a son is given, and the government will be on his shoulders. And he will be called wonderful counselor, mighty God, everlasting Father, Prince of peace. Of the increase of his government and peace, there will be no end. He will reign on David's throne and over his kingdom, establishing and upholding it from that time on and forever. The zeal for the LORD Almighty will accomplish this *(Isaiah 9:6–7)*.

Narrator 1/3: So, you see, God had planned that the Messiah, *(speak next phrase slowly and with emphasis)* the *promised one*, would be born to take away our sins. God keeps His promises.

Narrator 1: In the New Testament, we see this fulfilled when the angel Gabriel appears to a young Jewish girl, Mary, and tells her that she will bear the Christ child.

Angel Gabriel: The Holy Spirit will come upon you, and the power of the Most High will overshadow you. So, the holy one to be born will be called the Son of God. *(pause for 1 to 2 seconds before speaking loudly)* For nothing is impossible with God *(Luke 1:35–7)*.

Narrator 1: Even though Mary was not sure how this would happen, she believed the angel and said:

Mary: May it be to me as you have said.

Narrator 2: *(turn to the audience)* Do you know what the word Immanuel means? It means God with us *(In a loud voice)*. Just imagine. *(pause for 1 to 2 seconds before speaking the next phrase)* God with us!

Narrator 2 continues: Another remarkable fact is that Mary lived up in Galilee in the town of Nazareth. This is in northern Israel, by the Sea of Galilee. But anyone who studied the Old Testament prophecy knew that the Christ child would *not* be born in Nazareth. So, it was very interesting that Caesar Augustus issued a decree for a census. Every person had to travel to the place of their family home.

Narrator 1: Yes, according to the genealogies in Matthew and Luke, both Mary and Joseph were from David's family, so they needed to travel down to Bethlehem (David's home city) for the census. Shortly after they arrived, Mary gave birth to the baby, Jesus. Because the town was so crowded by the census, they could not find a place to stay. Everything was full up. So, the baby was born in a stable. And she wrapped him in cloths and laid him in a manger, the feeding trough for animals. Not the typical place for a king to be born!

Song suggestion: O Little Town of Bethlehem

Scene Three

Narrator 1/3: Not many people recognized the baby, Jesus, as the king of the Jews. However, there were some who did recognize the signs around them. You see, there was something special in the sky before the night Jesus was born. It was so special that people from the East started on a journey to follow it, looking for the King of the Jews so that they could worship him. They knew the promise from Balaam regarding Jacob's descendants.

Balaam: I see him, but not now; I behold him, but not nearby. A star will come out of Jacob; a scepter will rise out of Israel *(Numbers 14:17)*.

Narrator 2/4: *(turn to the audience)* This verse speaks about a star in the sky *and* of a ruler who will reign over the people of Israel. We know from other verses that it was necessary for Mary and Joseph to travel down to Bethlehem because of what Nathan told King David when the Word of the Lord came to Him;

Nathan: The LORD declares to you that the LORD himself will establish a house for you: When your days are over, and you rest with your fathers, I will raise up your offspring to succeed you, who will come from your own body, and I will establish his kingdom. He is the one who will build a house for my Name, and I will establish the throne of his kingdom forever *(2 Sam 7: 11–13)*.

Narrator 2: We know those seekers as the *magi* *(pronounced maj- eye)*. While the Magi were traveling to see the Christ child, they stopped in Jerusalem, at the king's palace, to enquire about the King of the Jews.

King Herod called together the Jewish chief priests and teachers of the law and asked them, "Where will this Christ be born?" They knew what was written long ago by the prophet Micah:

Micah: But you, Bethlehem Ephrathah, though you are small among the clans of Judah, out of you will come for me one who will be ruler over Israel, whose origins are from old, from ancient times *(Micah 5:2)*.

Song suggestion: It Came Upon a Midnight Clear

Narrator 2/4: Another truth in the book of Micah says:

Micah: He will stand and shepherd his flock in the strength of the Lord, in the majesty of the name of the Lord his God. And they will live securely, for then his greatness will reach to the ends of the earth. And he will be their peace *(Micah 5:4–5)*.

Who is a God like you, who pardons sin and forgives the transgression of the remnant of his inheritance? You do not stay angry forever but delight in showing mercy. You will again have compassion on us; you will tread our sins underfoot and hurl all our iniquities into the depths of the sea *(Micah 7:18–19)*.

Narrator 1: So, you see, that this promised one has a great task; to forgive our sins and to show mercy. I don't know about you, but I certainly need God's mercy every day.

The Jewish nation understood that the Messiah would come from David's family, so Herod asked the magi to send word back when they found the baby. But the magi were warned in a dream not to go back to Jerusalem, so they returned home by another route. And when Herod realized that he was tricked, he sent soldiers down to Bethlehem to kill all the baby boys under the age of two, the time the magi saw the star in the sky. His love of power was greater than his willingness to acknowledge the true king, Jesus. He was ruthless.

Fortunately, Joseph had a dream and listened to God regarding the baby, and they stole away in the night and fled to Egypt. God saved this baby Jesus from death because He had a special plan for his life; he was the Promised Messiah! God keeps His promise!

Conclusion:

Narrator: *(Use Narrator with strongest voice and confidence)* From the Bible, we learn that after Herod died, Jesus returned to Israel with his family and settled in Nazareth. When Jesus grew up, he became a rabbi, or teacher, to tell others about God's great love and compassion for His people. He was different from other teachers of the Law and was often misunderstood. In the end, he was killed on a cross, a cursed object. But this, too, was part of the plan because he rose from the dead. Today, Jesus is still fulfilling the promise of God to forgive sins and bring people back to God. So, you see, children, that Nativity is really the heart of Christmas and the *true* reason we celebrate Christmas.

That is why we should all have a Nativity to remind us

God keeps His promises!

Stage direction: *All take a bow!*

Needs for the Play

Title: **God Keeps His Promise**

[ ] Date of performance: ______________________

[ ] Date of practices: ____

Role	**Student**	**Alternate**	**comments**
Narrator 1			
Narrator 2			
God			
Abraham			
Isaiah			
Angel Gabriel			
Mary			
Baalam			
Nathan			
Micah			

[ ] Scripts printed off for children and adult leaders. The number needed: ______________

Additional needs for performance:

Stage/Lightening/sound:

[ ] costumes

[ ] microphones/ lighting, etc.

[ ] stage props, etc.

Songs/ Music:

[ ] Songs chosen

[ ] Music given to person organizing

[ ] one-page sheet written up for students

Who needs to know:

[ ] Confirm date with church calendar

[ ] Notice to parents

[ ] Advertisement to church and community

Role/student: ____________________

Play Four: Missing Christmas!

Scene One	Scene Two	Scene Three	Scene Four	Scene Five
Narrator	Narrator	Narrator	Narrator	Narrator
Innkeeper 1	Angel of Lord	Simeon	Magi 1	
Innkeeper 2	Host of Angels		Magi 2	
			Chief Priest	

Scene One: *the narrator comes onto the stage at one side. He gives meaning to each part as he watches on.*

Stage direction*: The choir should be placed to the side or back of the stage so they can easily step in to sing at the appropriate times.*

Narrator: *(Speak directly to the audience)* Today, I want to tell you a story that happened long, long ago. Even so, the message of the story is important for us today.

Many people in the old days in Israel were busy with work and the activities of daily life. They were much like you and me today. However, when a special person arrived, many people were so busy that they missed his birth *(pause for 1–2 seconds)*. They missed Christmas!

(Innkeepers enter to the opposite side of where the narrator is standing.)

Innkeeper 1: Do you remember when everyone had to travel to their hometown to register the census for Caesar Augustus? It was such a long time ago, and yet, *(pause for 1 to 2 seconds before saying softly)* I remember it as if it were yesterday.

Innkeeper 2: I remember that my inn was full for weeks; in fact, nearly every inn in Bethlehem was filled up to capacity for months. It was the best year for business. I do not think we have ever had a better year than that one. I heard that the innkeepers in Jerusalem, Emmaus and Bethany, were also thrilled to have so many people coming home for the census.

Innkeeper 1: It also put a great burden on the town. After traveling some distance, many people did not turn around and go back to the town or village that they had just left. It was not so easy to travel in those days. You had to take your entire family with you. Being a farming community, people were poor and did not have much money. So many of them found work and stayed around for a while to support their families after they arrived. Some stayed around for months and even years after they registered their family in the census.

Innkeeper 2: Yes, I remember one family who came that year. It was a young husband and his pregnant wife. They arrived very late in the day, and all my rooms were full up, just like all of the inns. I felt so bad for them I could not just turn them out, so I let them stay in the stable with the animals. They were happy enough just to have a place to stay out of the cold weather nights. I went to bed, feeling good that all my rooms were full up again! That was a good year!

Narrator: *(Speaking to the audience)* Yes, innkeepers were an important part of the community when Caesar Augustus issued the decree for the census *(Luke 2:1)*. With everyone moving across the country, there was a lot of traveling around, and people needed comfortable places to stay. But when Mary and Joseph, the parents of Jesus, came knocking at his door, the innkeeper did not know how important they were. They looked like many of the ordinary, poor people who were traveling because of the census. He missed an opportunity to share his home with them because he did not realize that the baby to be born was the savior of the Nation, the Messiah of his people. He went to bed *(Pause for 1 to 2 seconds)* and missed Christmas!

Song suggestion: O Come, O Come Emmanuel

Scene Two

Narrator: Even though the innkeeper missed his opportunity to welcome the baby Jesus, God had other plans. He sent his angels to announce the birth of Jesus in the region. Most people were sleeping comfortably in their beds that night, which seemed like any other night of the year. Shepherds, who were out in the fields with their sheep, were awakened by angels.

(Angels enter the stage on the opposite side to the Narrator.)

Angel of Lord: Do not be afraid. I bring you good news of great joy that will be for all the people. Today in the town of David, a Savior has been born to you; he is Christ the LORD. This will be a sign to you: You will find a baby wrapped in cloths and lying in a manger *(Luke 2:10–12)*.

Host of angels: Glory to God in the highest, and on earth peace to men on whom his favor rests *(Luke 2:14)*.

Narrator: The shepherds were amazed at what they heard. They did not usually go into town, but they decided to listen to the angels and went to town to check it out. They were surprised to find the baby, just as the angels said, lying in a manger. They told everyone about what they saw that night concerning the child. All were amazed; it seemed too good to be true. We do not know if the people believed, but they heard about the birth of Jesus that night. The shepherds were willing to go out of their way to investigate the news and were rewarded as the first to welcome the baby. They found Christmas!

Song suggestion: Angels We Have Heard on High

Scene Three

Narrator: In accordance with the Law, Joseph and Mary took the baby Jesus to the temple in Jerusalem to present him to the LORD because Every firstborn male is to be consecrated to the LORD *(Exodus 13:2,12)*. They provided the sacrifice of a poor person, a pair of doves, or two young pigeons. While there, Simeon, a devout and righteous man, came into the temple courts. He has been guided by the Holy Spirit to go that day. The Holy Spirit revealed to him that the baby was the Lord's, the Christ child. Simeon picked up the child and praised God:

Simeon: *(Hold up the baby Jesus doll above head with eyes raised to heaven)* My eyes have seen your salvation, which you have prepared in the sight of all people, a light for revelation to the Gentiles and for glory to your people Israel *(Luke 2:30)*.

Narrator: Mary and Joseph were amazed at what Simeon said about their child and pondered them for a long time. Simeon also blessed them and spoke directly to Mary:

Simeon: This child is destined to cause the falling and rising of many in Israel and to be a sign that will be spoken against so that the thoughts of many hearts will be revealed. And a sword will pierce your own soul too *(Luke 2:34,35)*.

Narrator: There was another person at the temple that day, an old prophetess, Anna, from the tribe of Asher. She also recognized something special about baby Jesus that day. She gave thanks to God and spoke about the child to anyone who was looking forward to the redemption of Jerusalem. Many listened and recognized the importance of this baby, the king of the Jews. They found Christmas.

Song suggestion: What Child is This?

Scene Four

Narrator: Sometime later, experts in the study of stars, the Magi *(pronounced Maj-eye),* arrived in Jerusalem, the place of worship for the Jews. We believe that they traveled a long distance, probably from Persia, and knew about the Old Testament prophecies regarding the Jewish Messiah they came seeking:

Magi 1: Where is the one who has been born king of the Jews?

Magi 2: Yes, we saw his star in the east and have come to worship him!

Narrator: Even though Jesus' birth took place in Bethlehem, only a few miles away, it seemed that no one in Jerusalem knew about it. But more importantly, no one was expecting it. King Herod asked the religious leaders of his time about the birth of the Christ child. They knew about the prophecy—

Chief priest: But you, Bethlehem, in the land of Judah, are by no means least among the rulers of Judah; for out of you will come a ruler who will be the shepherd of my people Israel *(Micah 5:2)*.

Narrator: So, the Magi traveled to Bethlehem and found the baby, just as Herod had informed them.

Isn't it interesting that the chief priests and teachers of the law who are supposed to know everything about the Messiah's birth did not see the special star in the sky and missed the birth of their King? Not only that, they were not curious about the Magi's message and made no effort to go down to Bethlehem to confirm the birth. They stayed in Jerusalem *(pause for 1 to 2 seconds)*. They missed Christmas!

Song Suggestion: O Little Town of Bethlehem

Scene Five: Final words

Narrator: It was long ago that Jesus became Emmanuel, God with us, born as a baby in that manager in Bethlehem. And just like then, today, there are some who still miss the importance of our yearly Christmas celebration of the birth of Jesus. They get caught up in the everyday activities of life and miss the most important message to us today. They do not recognize that Jesus is the promised Messiah who came to bring salvation to mankind if they would just believe in Jesus' finished work on the cross.

Stage direction: *speak slowly and directly to the audience*

Narrator: Please, do not be someone who misses Christmas!

Stage direction: *All take a bow!*

Recommendation: *Have the Pastor or other adult leader give a brief invitation to the audience for those who may want to know more about this important truth.*

Needs for the Play

Title: **Missing Christmas**

[ ] Date of performance: ______________________

[ ] Date of practices: ____

Role	**Student**	**Alternate**	**comments**
Narrator			
Innkeeper 1			
Innkeeper 2			
Angel of the Lord			
Host of angels			
Simeon			
Magi 1			
Magi 2			
Chief Priest			

[ ] Scripts printed off for children and adult leaders. The number needed: ______________

Additional needs for performance:

Stage/Lightening/sound:

[ ] costumes
[ ] microphones/ lighting, etc.
[ ] stage props, etc.

Songs/ Music:

[ ] Songs chosen
[ ] Music given to person organizing
[ ] one-page sheet written up for students

Who needs to know:

[ ] Confirm date with church calendar
[ ] Notice to parents
[ ] Advertisement to church and community

From the Hillside

Hark the Herald Angel Sing
Hark! The herald angels sing,
glory to the newborn king;
Peace on earth, and mercy mild,
God and sinners reconciled!
Joyful all ye nations rise,
join the triumph of the skies;
With angelic host proclaim,
Christ is born in Bethlehem!
Hark the herald angels sing,
Glory to the newborn King.

Christ by highest heav'n adored
Christ the everlasting Lord!
Late in time behold Him come,
Offspring of the Virgin's womb.
Veiled in flesh the Godhead see
Hail th'incarnate De-I-ty.
Pleased as man with men to dwell
Jesus, our Emmamuel.
Hark! The herald angels sing,
Glory to the newborn King.

Away in a Manger
(first verse- toddlers only)
1..Away in a manger
No crib for a bed
The little Lord Jesus
Laid down his sweet head.
The stars in the bright sky
Looked down where He lay
The little Lord Jesus asleep
on the hay.

(all students sing rest of verses)
2. The cattle are lowing
The baby awakes
The little Lord Jesus
No crying he makes
I love thee, Lord Jesus
Look down from the sky
And stay by my cradle
'Til morning is nigh.

3. Be near be, Lord Jesus
I ask thee to stay
Close by me forever
And love me, I pray.
Bless all the dear children
In they tender care,
And fit us for heaven
To live with thee there.

Angels We Have Heard on High
1. Angel we have heard on high
Sweetly singing o're the plain
And the mountains in reply
Echoing their joyous strain

Chorus:
Gloria. In excels Deo.
Gloria. In excels Deo

2. Shepherd, why this jubilee?
Why you joyous strains prolong?
Say what may the tidings be,
Which inspire your heavenly song?
Chorus:

3. Come to Bethlehem and see
Him whose birth the angels sing;
Come, adore on bended knee
Christ the Lord, the newborn King.
Chorus:

4. See within a manager laid,
Jesus, Lord of heav'n and earth!
Mary, Joseph lend your aid,
With us sing the Savior's birth.
Chorus:

Go Tell It on the Mountain
Chorus:
Go tell it on the mountain
Over the hills and everywhere
Go tell it on the mountain
That Jesus Christ is born

While Shepherds kept their watching
O'er silent flocks by night,
Behold thr'out the heavens
There shone a holy light.

Chorus-

The shepherd feared and trembled
When lo! Above the earth
Rang out the angel chorus
That hailed our Savior's birth.

Chorus-

Down in a lowly manger
The humble Christ was born
And brought us God's salvation
That blessed Christmas morn.
Chorus-

O Little Town of Bethlehem
1. O little town of Bethlehem
How still we see thee lie!
Above thy deep and dreamless sleep
The silent stars go by
Yet in they dark streets shineth
The everlasting Light
The hopes and fears of all the years
Are met in thee tonight.

4. O holy child of Bethlehem
Descend on us, we pray
Cast out our sin and enter in
Be born in us today
We hear the Christmas angels
The great glad tidings tell
O come to us, abide with us
Our Lord, Emmanuel.

Joy to the World!
1. Joy to the world! The Lord is come.
Let earth receive her king.
Let every heart prepare HIM room
And heav'n and nature sing,
And heav'n and nature sing,
And heav'n and heav'n and nature
sing.

2. Joy to the world! The Savior reigns
Let men their songs employ.
While fields and floods,
Rocks, hills and plains
Repeat the sounding joy,
Repeat the sounding joy,
Repeat, repeat the sounding joy.

4. He rules the world with truth and grace
And makes the nations prove
The glories of his righteousness
And wonders of His love
And wonders of His love,
And wonders, wonders of His love.

One Starry Night

It Came Upon a Midnight Clear

It came upon the midnight clear,
That glorious song of old,
From angels bending near the earth,
To touch their harps of gold;
"Peace on the earth, good will to men,
From Heav'n's all-gracious King."
The world in solemn stillness lay
To hear the angels sing.

Still through the cloven skies they come
With peaceful wings unfurled,
And still their heav'nly music floats
O'er all the weary world;
Above its sad and lowly plains,
They bend on hov'ring wing,
And ever o'er its Babel sounds
The blessed angels sing.

For lo! the days are hast'ning on,
By prophet seen of old,
When with the ever-circling years
Shall come the time foretold
When Christ shall come and all
shall own
The Prince of Peace, their King,
And saints shall meet Him in the air,
And with the angels sing.

Away in a Manger

Away in a manger
No crib for a bed
The little Lord Jesus
Laid down his sweet head.
The stars in the bright sky
Looked down where He lay
The little Lord Jesus asleep
on the hay.

The cattle are lowing
The baby awakes
The little Lord Jesus
No crying he makes
I love thee, Lord Jesus
Look down from the sky
And stay by my cradle
'Til morning is nigh.

Be near be, Lord Jesus
I ask the to stay
Close by me forever
And love me, I pray.
Bless all the dear children
In thy tender care,
And fit us for heaven
To live with thee there.

God Keeps His Promise

Away in a Manger

1. Away in a manger
No crib for a bed
The little Lord Jesus
Laid down his sweet head.
The stars in the bright sky
Looked down where He lay
The little Lord Jesus asleep
on the hay.

2. The cattle are lowing
The baby awakes
The little Lord Jesus
No crying he makes
I love thee, Lord Jesus
Look down from the sky
And stay by my cradle
'Til morning is nigh.

3. Be near be, Lord Jesus
I ask thee to stay
Close by me forever
And love me, I pray.
Bless all the dear children
In they tender care,
And fit us for heaven
To live with thee there.

O Come All Ye Faithful

O come all ye faithful
Joyful and triumphant
O come ye, o come ye to Bethlehem
Come and behold Him
Born the King of angels
O come, let us adore Him
O come, let us adore Him
O come, let us adore Him
Christ the Lord

Sing choirs of angels
Sing in exultation
O sing all ye citizens
Of heaven above
Glory to God
Glory in the highest
O come, let us adore Him
O come, let us adore Him
O come, let us adore Him
Christ the Lord
Yeah Lord, we greet Thee
Born this happy morning
Jesus to Thee be all glory
Word of the Father
Now in flesh appearing
O come, let us adore Him
O come, let us adore Him
O come, let us adore Him
Christ the Lord

Optional ending:

You are the Lord
You are the Lord
You are the Lord, yeah
We'll praise Your name forever
We'll praise Your name forever
We'll praise Your name forever
Christ the Lord
Glory in the highest
We'll praise Your name forever
We'll praise Your name forever
We'll praise Your name forever
Christ the Lord

O Little Town of Bethlehem

1. O little town of Bethlehem
How still we see thee lie!
Above thy deep and dreamless sleep
The silent stars go by
Yet in they dark streets shineth
The everlasting Light
The hopes and fears of all the years
Are met in thee tonight.

4. O holy child of Bethlehem
Descend on us, we pray
Cast out our sin and enter in
Be born in us today
We hear the Christmas angels
The great glad tidings tell
O come to us, abide with us
Our Lord, Emmanuel.

It Came Upon a Midnight Clear

It came upon the midnight clear,
That glorious song of old,
From angels bending near the earth,
To touch their harps of gold;
"Peace on the earth, good will to men,
From Heav'n's all-gracious King."
The world in solemn stillness lay,
To hear the angels sing.

Still through the cloven skies they come,
With peaceful wings unfurled,
And still their heav'nly music floats
O'er all the weary world;
Above its sad and lowly plains,
They bend on hov'ring wing,
And ever o'er its Babel sounds
The blessed angels sing.

Yet with the woes of sin and strife
The world has suffered long;
Beneath the angel strain have rolled
Two thousand years of wrong;
And man, at war with man, hears not
The love-song which they bring;
Oh, hush the noise, ye men of strife
And hear the angels sing.

And ye, beneath life's crushing load,
Whose forms are bending low,
Who toil along the climbing way
With painful steps and slow,
Look now! for glad and golden hours
Come swiftly on the wing.
Oh, rest beside the weary road,
And hear the angels sing!

For lo! the days are hast'ning on,
By prophet seen of old,
When with the ever-circling years
Shall come the time foretold
When Christ shall come and all shall own
The Prince of Peace, their King,
And saints shall meet Him in the air,
And with the angels sing.

Missing Christmas

O Come, O Come Emmanuel

O come, O come, Emmanuel
And ransom captive Israel
That mourns in lonely exile here
Until the Son of God appear
Rejoice! Rejoice! Emmanuel
Shall come to thee, O Israel

O come, Thou Key of David, come
And open wide our heavenly home
Make safe the way that leads on high
And close the path to misery
Rejoice! Rejoice! Emmanuel
Shall come to thee, O Israel

O come, Thou Wisdom from on high
And order all things, far and nigh
To us the path of knowledge show
And cause us in her ways to go
Rejoice! Rejoice! Emmanuel
Shall come to thee, O Israel

O come, desire of nations, bind
In one the hearts of all mankind
Bid Thou our sad divisions cease
And be Thyself our King of peace
Rejoice! Rejoice! Emmanuel
Shall come to thee, O Israel

Angels We Have Heard on High

1. Angel we have heard on high
Sweetly singing o're the plain
And the mountains in reply
Echoing their joyous strain

Chorus:
Gloria. In excels Deo.
Gloria. In excels Deo

2. Shepherd, why this jubilee?
Why your joyous strains prolong?
Say what may the tidings be,
Which inspire your heavenly song?
Chorus:

3. Come to Bethlehem and see
Him whose birth the angels sing;
Come, adore on bended knee
Christ the Lord, the newborn King.
Chorus:

4. See within a manager laid,
Jesus, Lord of heav'n and earth!
Mary, Joseph lend your aid,
With us sing the Savior's birth.
Chorus:

What child is this?

What child is this who laid to rest
On Mary's lap is sleeping?
Whom angels greet with anthems sweet
While the good shepherds watch are keeping

So, bring Him incense, gold, and myrrh
Come peasant, king to own Him
The King of Kings salvation brings
Let loving hearts enthrone Him

This, this is Christ the King
Whom shepherds guard and angels sing
Haste, haste to bring Him laud
The babe, the son of Mary

O Little Town of Bethlehem

1. O little town of Bethlehem
How still we see thee lie!
Above thy deep and dreamless sleep
The silent stars go by
Yet in they dark streets shineth
The everlasting Light
The hopes and fears of all the years
Are met in thee tonight.

4. O holy child of Bethlehem
Descend on us, we pray
Cast out our sin and enter in
Be born in us today
We hear the Christmas angels
The great glad tidings tell
O come to us, abide with us
Our Lord, Emmanuel.

Printed in the USA
CPSIA information can be obtained
at www.ICGtesting.com
LVHW082041281024
795041LV00005B/81

9 798887 387031